AF200466

J.C. Manto

still cheaper

than therapy

poems

Bibliografische Information der Deutschen Nationalbibliothek:
Die Deutsche Nationalbibliothek verzeichnet diese Publikation in
der Deutschen Nationalbibliografie; detaillierte bibliografische
Daten sind im Internet über dnb.dnb.de abrufbar.

Herstellung und Verlag: BoD – Books on Demand, Norderstedt

Cover und Layout © Traumstoff Buchdesign traumstoff.at
Motive © olgasoi007 shutterstock.com
Illustration *the storm* © J.C. Manto

ISBN: 978-3-7504-0286-7

#intro

6

About

J.C. Manto alias Claudia Toman is a writer, designer, photographer, feminist, resister and geek from Vienna, Austria. She has published half a dozen novels under her real name and the pen name Anna Koschka, designs book covers for a living and writes poetry to survive.

A while ago I sat in the auditorium of Wiener Konzerthaus and listened to Amanda Palmer singing and telling stories of her life. I tried my best not to think the obvious thought: that I had avoided this place, the whole area for four years. It was the last place my dad went before he died. He had a ticket for a concert in his pocket, they handed it to me with all his other belongings. I'll never know what happened that day. He must have fallen on the way from the car to the concert hall. Someone found him lying on the pavement and called an ambulance. He was in intensive care for two weeks when his heart suddenly stopped. They couldn't explain it to me. Except that there were a lot of medical conditions that somehow multiplied. He never fully woke up in those two weeks and I wasn't able to talk to him. I was in therapy for over a year just to get to the point where I could accept that I had *never* talked to him. In all our life together we had never had a real conversation about pain and pride and loss. You see, my mum had died of cancer when I was five. Dad and I, we both never healed. We just lived side by side in our individual bubbles. So when he died I was left alone. A singular bubble. And because there are no coincidences in life the day before he fell, the last day of my old life, Amanda Palmer published her song *Bigger on the Inside*. I remember lying in the dark with my headphones on listening to it.

In the weeks that came after the end, the song was my companion. Everything I felt and couldn't put into words was there in the deep, profound sound of the cello, the hyperventilating ukulele and the fragility and boldness of Amanda's voice.

So it was really fitting that the first time I dared to visit the spot where my dad had never arrived at was for an Amanda Palmer concert. And not long after the opening she told us the story of how her parents replaced the strings of the piano she was wildly playing on as a kid without complaining because they figured it was still cheaper than therapy. And it struck me then and there. I had been writing poetry for about a year, it was me trying to find my way back to being a writer, an ability I had lost completely with loss and grief. Therapy hadn't brought it back and I was stuck, because it was too expensive to talk to this stranger week after week. But suddenly I knew what I wanted to do with this weird collection of poems. They are very personal and at the same time I think that everybody who has been at the pinnacle of grief, depression, anxiety or addiction will be able to relate. And in any case, reading them is still cheaper than therapy, so it won't hurt to give it a try.

9

#doesit
bring
youjoy

the art of tidying up

does it bring you joy?
asked a crash test marie kondo
at the switchboard of my brain.
and i looked at the reflection
of myself in knickers, bra, and pain.

not in a while i said
and dropped the underwear,
unbuttoned the skin
from the back of my neck
down to my heels
and threw it in the bin.

Inspired by my Patron Anja Bayer

13

naught

it's always dawn
on the island of couch
never sun, never moon
just a constant notquite
and somehow my eyes
have adapted to the light
never open, never closed
dark circles, puffed pouch
automaton.

this lack of drive
is obstructing the view
never sea, never land
just a volatile naught
and somehow my heart
has adapted to the drought
never empty, never full
a room with a queue
barely alive.

Inspired by my Patron Sonja Meißl-Ulreich

shell

hold the thread
don't pull
the caterpillar spins
eight hundred yards
of pure silk just to
get a pair of wings.

can you hear them grow?
microscopically small
scales in a
microscopically small world.

she doesn't feel it
if you kill her
boiling water
steaming hot, only
the wings stop
growing and a
never ever lingers
in the cocoon.

magic

the old witch at the
end of the road
never conjures, she rips
grey cardboard in
pieces thick as fingers and
fills the room with
frayed ends, the
silence between the
blind spots and the rugged
fibrousness of naught.

at times i see her
through dusty glass
dreaming magic on lips
voiceless and soft
as if she was younger and
not a book with
frayed ends in
chambers under the
anguish and the hundred
facial masks of fraud.

ache

i took a sip of storm in the
morning, the colour of the
sky a pale bluish green
cascades of winter in the
air and an amber lostness in my
cup of extra strong gale
seething slowly at the back of my
mouth, flavour of leaves
clinging to trees lest it
hurts too much to fall or be
blown away, but still
aching like hell
to fly.
to fly.

autumn

her tomcat answers to
twenty-eight pet names
he's old like her
and cautious when he's
crossing the street
and sometimes when he
sleeps curled up by the window
at sunset
she calls him autumn
and together they dream
of summer

a life collected in
twenty-eight volumes
who came, who went
the law of nature
withering growth
and sometimes when she
counts frostwork on the window
at sunset
she's warmed by autumn
one last time before
the winter

contact

have you ever waited
for someone to call
or answer your text,
like your tweet,
write on your wall?
took your phone,
microwaved it,
watched it explode?
sat in the dark
because you couldn't
remember the code
for the payphone
you own, being all smart
to call an electrician
who'd fix the light
and your broken heart?
have you ever walked
all alone at night
to a phone booth
or a shop selling fuses
and told yourself: right,
this is not the worst
only seemed so at first?

Inspired by my Patron Ivonne Keller

lost

i have a ring
i never take off
zero point six three
sterling silver
fits me perfectly
only sometimes it slips
off my finger at night
and i wake up
drenched in sweat
with a terrible fright
that it's lost
or somehow replaced
with a cheap reproduction
zero point six two
metal clay
fixed with some glue
always too small
always a fake
like the skin that i live in
while i'm awake.

awkward dance

i stood on my toes
for most of our
conversation
like a ballet dancer
in heavy boots
only without those
graceful moves
doing pirouettes
like a downy birch
with stunted roots
just so you'd like me
just so you'd know
the foolish things i'd do:
i'd cut my heel
or grow a wheel
under each toe
to fit in your shoe.

dragon's flight

flat on my back
and looking up
the sky was red
and scaled with
killmenots

you've never heard
of those, you say?

tightly they are
woven and look
like something burnt
all flecked with
tiny dots.

they don't exist
except in dreams?

but what if they
are all there is
between the two:
your fire
and my shots.

Inspired by my Patron Kristina Hampl

#love
poems

yellow

i once had a lump
the size of my fist
they didn't see it on x-rays
it wasn't a cyst.

and yet there it was
right under my skin
how did it get there, i wondered?
and stuck in a pin.

at first there was pain
like i've never felt
at least the force of an air crash
with no safety belt.

but soon i got used
to my benign growth
and started giving it pet names
while making an oath.

it wasn't until
we didn't agree
an epiphanic realization:
the lump now had me.

red

the sanguine moon rose
roughly when my hand chose
to touch the ghost of yours
on a doorknob and then sank.

i tunnelled my way
through the asphalt and clay
to where no light invades,
there i curled up and then shrank.

i didn't come out
of the hole for about
the time it took the moon
to roll flushed off the plank.

crimson

'magic, do as you will,'
she said like schmendrick once
and asked the brick walls
for advice,
her heart painted
in crimson red
with sailor moon eyes
and the devil's front teeth.

'no gps in love'
(the voice of mickey mouse)
'receive a signal
or turn around'
(she recognized the house)

'why is there a hole
in superwoman's heart?'
she wanted to know
and hid her face behind her
cape of crimson red,
trained in the art
of losing inner organs
to the bullet underneath.

green

because i'm getting old
from my middle years
i write your name
(as a precaution)
in capital letters
on the wall, so
that i keep it in mind
even if you can't remember
mine, you see
my love won't age with me
it just grows more branched
like a box tree in a park
loses its shape
but remains itself unaltered
and if i die
the writing might fade
or the wall collapse
that's highly possible
these days, but
at least it's an attempt
to preserve something so
fleeting as this moment
for some sort of
evermore.

tan

peel the skin
from your september sickness
until the blood washes out.

find your way
through the old and narrow streets
follow the silk thread by heart.

smell of wood
and cracked leather burning
like every fire undoused.

we're two sides
of something underrated
that i cannot live without.

acid

the noise of your
possible reaction
won't ever stop
it's a constant static
twentyfourseven
entotic murmur
drop after drop:
the rain falling
on my overgrown mind
and i know you
as well as myself
our fingers lined
with a pinch of salt
and a terrible thirst
what would you do?
i'm not asking.
let me gif you first.

Inspired by my Patron Michaela Dorninger

white

the spot where the needle
stung your moon into my night
won't heal, it's scabbing in
layers of light and dark
broken through the blinds
on my pillow where i lay
dreaming of you turning your
head in slow-motion to a
song by nick cave.
that's how deep the ink seeped in.
i bled in the rain, fled in the sun and
shred myself in the hail.
it's where you scarred me
that i hurt
the least.

gray

sometimes i try you on
like a coat of all the
things i made up woven with
fragments of images
you use to describe yourself.

a faint smell of brick and
wine stained coasters on a
table i didn't lay in a
house i do not live in
east of where i won't ever stay.

no, i don't think you
see me or feel the way my
freezing hands slip into the
sleeves of your
pitch-feathered skin.

underneath it's just a
lion roaring with a polished
heart of tin.

black

on the rim of twilight
sits a magpie
with just one eye
and if you ask her
how a dream is made
you get two nights of pleasure
and one bad wreck.

and that's what love must be:
twice flying
once abyss
and if you ask me
what desire's like,
you get two snow-white feathers
and one that's black.

the storm

you never chased the storm
you made it
you brewed the sea
in a chipped cup
until it spilled
and flooded the room
that was left in me.
i never fled the storm
i drank it.

Inspired by Toby Stephens

#weneed another wordfor over

page

your part in my story
is like one of those pages
in wreck this journal
where explicit instructions
tell you the method
to ruin the sheet.

i folded the edges
as it said in the manual
the boat of paper
like in stephen king's novel
swirled in the water
then sank in the street.

it left me distracted
for there is no tutorial
on how to pick up
all the words never written
scattered like chain links
where we never meet.

Inspired by my Patron Ursula Poznanski

41

13

thirteen steps
from the terrace
of kiyomizu-dera
to the ground
if you jump
so they say
your every wish will
be fulfilled.

thirteen years
i have known you
abyss always conspicuous
never jumped
never fell
just wishes
carved deeply into
rotten wood.

thirteen words
more or less so
a parting like a drop of
soya sauce
you and me
we've done our best to
go amiss.

pain

on the outside
not a ripple
deep dead water
calm as clam.

underneath it
feel the abscess
holding on to
what i am.

all the while a
constant swelling
blood and pus
in need of sting.

and i wonder
if i lost you
would the pain be
blistering?

i will be

i will still be writing poems for you
at my desk between piles of old papers
i'll never read
after searching my glasses for half an hour
with narrow eyes
the flowers on my frock
a faded shade of lavender.
i will be starting them with *if*
and end them on *remember.*

i will still be painting crooked lines
on the canvas of your face at night
before i go to sleep
after five and a half failed attempts
with hands still shaking
the glow on my cheek
something close to forever.
i will be clearing them with *since*
and darken them with *oh, but never.*

#aroom ofmyown

the emperor

tear the land to
tiny little pieces and
beat your time with
tiny little hands, until your
lies seep out of tiny little
pores, you won't bequeath
anything but slack
threads, your legacy a
crack in your own
front, unaware of it
collapsing, because of the
tiny little letters you fudge to
tiny little thoughts, the
emperor's new tweet and
everyone but you can
see your nought, when
your own rabidness
tears you to bits.

john doe

the snow-white wolf
was master of the forest
his reign was long
and prosperous
in fact
he spent his time
admiring the reflection
of snow white hair
in fearful eyes
the act
elaborate
a master of deception
he preyed in daylight
so obvious
but yet
the songbirds hushed
he built them silver cages
their pain was locked
conveniently
a threat:
the wolf was smart
and knew just what to tell them
his promise sound
the menace gag
your choice!

but he forgot
there's one bird in the forest
who'll sing his song
nevertheless:
one voice.
the snow-white wolf
predator of the forest
had snow white teeth
and piercing eyes
pale blue
one day he woke
the cages all were empty
and in the sky
a flock of birds.
#metoo!

Inspired by I.H.

bomb

excuse my accent, i don't speak fluent
misogynist or male agenda for i am in fact
a woman, i have been paid less, told to get
married for my worth and learn to cook and
always, always do the dishes after.
i have been touched without consent,
hands on my hair, my breasts,
my ass and my growing anger.
i have never been touched like that
by a woman not even
the one who really fell in love with me
when we sat in that hotel bar in tel aviv
and talked about bombs and men
and men who were like bombs.

did i mention the man who was
married and thirty years older than me?
who cheerfully told me the story
of a girl he once fucked,
who looked like twenty-five
makeup, high heels, sexy outfit and all
but actually she was fourteen and
his eyes lit up with smug complacency

fourteen for christ's sake and when he
joked about it in the cafeteria
his workmates laughed and
their laughter sounded like bombs
ticking in a leather suitcase
filled with fake plastic penises.

men explained shit to me like
phone chargers, woody allen movies, brexit
and even my own vagina
they have told me that it is my own
fault if my body makes them horny,
excuse my french, mate, this is my
body and it doesn't make you
wolf whistle or get a boner or give you an
excuse to throw the bomb my way
just because i choose to shave my
legs and wear a skirt on a friday night
on leicester square, no,
it is your fucking bomb.
eat it up or blow it out!

room

i am she and he
and her and him
i don't wait for you
to write me a poem
or sing me a song
i am mine and yours
and nobody's at all
and if i want to
i will buy you roses
and it's not wrong
to have a room
with a door
and a lock
and a key
where i sit
and write a poem
just for me.

#poems
iwrotein
bookshops

task

sometimes i write
notes to strangers
and hide them
between the pages
of banana yoshimoto
or virginia woolf.
i spend a lot of time
in bookshops
it's the smell i like
and reading nooks
by the window
but most of all
the thought of you,
some stranger,
finding a note
between the pages
of banana yoshimoto
or virginia woolf.
if you ever see me
with a piece of paper
climbing out of
a bookshelf, don't ask!
just wait until i've
left you with the story,
find the book,
that is your task!

wrap

the book just sat there on a shelf
in the bookshop on piccadilly
and when my fingers
touched the
safety plastic wrap
i remembered how you
read it to me
and what it meant to you
and that you liked your coffee
so strong and sweet
that one time you spilled it
because it made you sneeze.
the stain never came off
the cover of the book
i remembered how that
made you cry and i thought of
buying you a new copy
but for some reason i never did.
i don't know what happened
to the book after you died.

it must have ended up
on the clearance pile
or gotten lost with time and there
in the bookshop on piccadilly
an old familiar coffee stain
made me realize that
everything we lose
is still wrapped in plastic
somewhere.

dream

there's a bookshop
next to my door
where the books are ordered
according to the dreams
they are for.
some i have read
from end to end
and i touch them gently
as though they are buildings
made of sand.
others i've missed
all of my life
i cry through the preface
break in the middle and
part at strife.
you are the one
i've yet to find
in your shoes i have strayed
your pages i've turned, just
in my mind.

#poems
iwrote
instead
ofkilling
myself

59

no one, joan!

the truth is
no one will save you
from killing yourself, joan!
they will be
shocked and bewildered
but how could they have known?

except that
your signals were red
just like blood on wet stone.
but people
tend to believe that
it will be okay, joan!

a choice, ophelia!

counting string lights
in the water
ten dots like brushstrokes
on a canvas
black as the inside
of a fox's den.

simple pattern
on the surface
my body shaking
cold and marbly
white as the hair tips
of a fox's tail.

a reflection
of the night sky
the only lifebuoy
within arm's reach
red as the trickle
from the fox's wound.

god

a life for a life
said the dust god
you can't save
anything or anyone.
for the fledgling
you fish out of the pond
another one will
fall out of the nest
you see?
a death is a death
so live with it!
you won't cheat
anything or anyone.
when they found me
face down in the pond
i think i heard a
chirp up in the nest
you see?
a life for a life
there is no god
who could save
anything or anyone.

praying mantis

i want to die
so badly
not kill myself
just cease to
exist.

you know, like a
praying mantis
on the doorstep
whose lifespan
is up.

i lie on my back
exhausted
and wait for a
voice that says
dismissed.

so i can finally
rest my palps
and stop sipping
fear from this
paper cup.

it's all rubbish!

if i die
it has to be in london
hit by a garbage truck
somewhere in soho.
that's highly specific
said my therapist
i smiled with a shrug
and said i know:
there is something poetic
about the fact that london
kills me with her clutter
as though
all the years i have loved her
were piled up bin bags
on the pavement
somewhere in soho.

#cheaper thantherapy

art

in the summer
that wasn't
i woke up each day
and walked down
the hill
from maybe to doesn't
picking up words
like pebbles
dropping out of my
headphones
precisely one hundred
as though meant for drabbles
which never made sense
so remained unwritten
instead they piled up
on my chest
like pavers
everybody was smitten
by the weightiness
of pain
as installed by
the artist who couldn't.

stranger

all the faces you see
on an average day
in the streets of the city
all the things you hear them say
like avocado wraps
and booby traps
and all the time you know
you're not one of them
you just pretend
with your fists clenched
biting your lips
until they bleed.

Inspired by my Patron Berta Berger

knight of the woeful countenance

fight me, said the windmill
and swung her arms
in perfect circles
around my head.
you're just a giant problem
i replied and knew
before she killed me
that i was dead.

loser, neighed the lame horse
who do you think
you're fooling
with all that blood?
stand up, you giant chicken,
brush your beak
and pick your crumbs
out of the mud!

hunger

walking through vineyards
on top of the hill
first day of fall
i stole some grapes
every now and then
truth is, i wanted them all
with every sweetness
i sensed on my tongue
i deeply yearned
to eat every single one
that was ever grown
since the earth first turned
it was a hunger
i had never felt
a desperate need
for an endless supply
of that tickling sensation
and a vicious greed
every grape in the world
would not be enough
i had to have more
now i'll never see vineyards
quite in the same way
as i did before.

i

separated
we were born
you left
an hour after dawn
nobody saw you
but me and her
she kept the secret
then and there
half a name
was my due
your memory
a shade of blue
absentee
and connate eye
the vowel
so close to why.

Inspired by my Patron Kirsten Greco

zombie

some nights i grab
a pair of scissors
to cut my toenails
and then my toes.
the bleeding's brisk
ruins the carpet
seeps into woodwork
where nothing grows.

how does it feel
i often wonder
to cut one leg off?
or both of them?
bleeding to life
could resurrect them
they'd walk on woodwork
without my phlegm.

grief

if you have a garden
sometimes on rare occasions
you see something bloom
but most of the time
you end up burying things
under the bushes in a tomb.

you never get used to
death and its stiff fragility
in dull broken eyes
but most of the time
you end up bracing your heart
under the surface telling lies.

hapsichord drabble

when they met,
she sat on the moon
and he wore a rainy day
around his neck
eating cake
out of a plastic box
while someone danced
to a silver lining
and the red door
of the coffee shop
was closed.

all of a sudden,
her heart leapt for joy
and all the vinegar and sea salt
in her wounds.

when she pushed the button,
they kissed and she drowned,
like a movie with the soundtrack
of a hapsichord slightly out of tune.

she paused and took the headphones off.
'I'll buy the record' she said
and paid in cash.

jet-black lining

i went to a bar
in soho once
and had a drink
they called
suspicious activity.
it came with a wish
in a bottle of storm
and a core of
white chocolate
autumn rain.

and i still recall
the aftertaste
it left me full
of clouds
and i spilled it on purpose.
but how come a wish
in a bottle of storm
could burn my sky
and leave a
jet-black stain?

amanda

buying quills is still
cheaper than therapy,
i thought
and better than lying.

so i drew faces
i could not forget
on sketch blocks
in tears.

only in plain ink
apparently
but just close enough
to actually crying.

making art is still
cheaper than therapy,
i thought,
and better than dying

so i wrote a poem
about the day
i committed
suicide.

only in my mind
apparently
but just close enough
to actually trying.

and i believe that
in some other timeline
i might have cried.
i might have died.
given up the fight.

but that's not my job,
she told me as she
walked into the dark
if you can, you must
make some light.

Inspired by Amanda Palmer

Thank you

Every writer needs one thing most of all: Inspiration. There are days when it seems impossible to ever write again. When the island of couch is stuck in the doldrums. Thank you **Toby Stephens** for the storm, for James and for allowing me to make art based on your talent. Me writing again wouldn't have been possible without you. And thank you **Amanda Palmer** for your music and teaching me the art of asking and giving. This is my job.

Love and thanks to my partner **Philipp** and my friends **Victoria** and **Judith** for putting up with me in good and bad times. You are my rocks and roots.

A big thank you to my English correctors **Tiffany Beasley** and **Jennifer Pruess**! And my proof reader **Zhenya Matysiak.**

And of course this book could not have been made without the support and inspiration of my patrons on Patreon. I'm so glad that I have you! Special thanks you to my power dragons **Ivonne Keller, Ursula Poznanski, Corina Bomann, Kristina Hampl, Berta Berger, Anja Bayer, Sonja Meißl-Ulreich, Doris Schaumberger and Christian von Aster!**

And the rest of the lovely dragon hoard: Julia Ilg, Astrid Dirnberger, Barbara Gruber, Birgit Borloni, Carola Wijsman, Charlie Lyne, Hilke-Gesa Bußmann, Ingrid Kerndtner, Isa Theobald, Jana Seidel, Julia Abrahams, Kirsten Greco, Klaudia Jilch, Mascha Vassena, Michaela Dorninger, Peter Bosch, Petra Balke-Besser, Sabrina Siebert, Sarah Hachmeister, Sonja Birgmann, Sylvie Grohne, Victoria Schlederer and Sarah Dörkes.

And a big shoutout to the *Black Sails* fandom on the internet and my Walrus Crew. If you haven't watched this show, watch it! It inspires poetry.

If you want to support me, please follow me on Patreon: www.patreon.com/shippingdragons